IDENTITY THEFT

IDENTITY THEFT

DON'T BE A VICTIM

www.identitytheftdontbeavictim.com

KEITH STODDART
AFROUZ NIKMANESH

K & A Publishing
Irvine, CA 92612

Printed in the United States of America

ISBN 978-0-578-04330-2

CONTENTS

PREFACE

Identity theft can not only cost you time and money, but it can ruin your credit and destroy your good name.

E VERY day we hear that identity (ID) theft is the fastest-growing crime in the U.S. We receive booklets, brochures, e-mails, and letters on how to protect ourselves and what to do when it happens.

It is almost like getting cancer—we assume that it happens to everyone else, but will never happen to us. The truth of the matter is that we are all vulnerable, and when it does hit we are lost. We get angry, feel violated, and then desperate. We start running around with no direction and feel completely lost. Believe me; *I* have been there.

Because I learned a lot about ID theft on my road to recovery from it, I decided to write an easy-to-read booklet with easy-to-follow instructions as to exactly what it takes to protect yourself—and in case you do become a victim—how to rectify your situation.

This is a global problem, so I will also provide tips for

those of you who travel overseas; I will let you know what to do before you start your journey and what to do during your trip to protect yourself.

So please keep this book somewhere handy. You never know when you will need it. It contains pertinent information such as phone numbers, websites, and sources you can rely on to get you out of the disaster that is called: *identity theft*.

CHAPTER 1

HOW IT ALL BEGAN

WHEN I received my credit card statement back in October of 2006 and it was unusually high, I knew something was wrong. One thousand dollars was withdrawn from my card somewhere in Wisconsin. I live in California and have never even been to Wisconsin. I called the Credit Card Company immediately, and I was told not to worry about it. They credited my account right away, and I never heard from them again.

No one warned me that this could be the beginning of a disaster, and that I should investigate it further. No one informed me that I should take some precautionary steps to avoid more headaches in the future.

A few months later I used the same credit card, and it was rejected. I called the credit card company to find out why. This time it was more than just bad news or a minor inconvenience; it was a disaster. My identity had been stolen—only this time the thieves had waited two months to strike again.

This time the credit card company did not simply credit my account. This time the credit card company needed proof that *I* was *me*! Apparently, a man had called the credit card company just a few weeks before, requesting a new credit card in my name. Incredibly, the credit card company had actually sent it to him at *a completely different address* than the one on my file! Nobody at the company had bothered to call the phone number on my profile to make sure that *I* was the person who had made the request.

I am a *female* and was the only one on the account, and yet the card company had sent out a new credit card in my name to a different address at the request of a *man*. Later, the company had noticed suspicious activities on my account, and had put a hold on it—still never bothering to call *me* about it. It was unbelievable.

And now the client service representative was telling *me*, the actual account holder, that *I* had to prove *I* was who *I* claimed to be. It took me almost a whole week and exactly thirty-two phone calls to convince them that *I* was *me*. I had to send them copies of my social security card, driver's license, credit card, and utility bills showing my mailing address. Meanwhile they were being extremely difficult; they would not even accept certain utility bills, such as my water bill.

That's when the run-around started.

I repeatedly called the fraud department at the credit card company, but they would not release any information regarding the activities on the card. They would not even tell me how I could protect myself against the consequences of the theft. Finally, after almost a week of going back and forth, they decided to believe me.

However, by this time, the thief had already begun

using my identity. The thought of my ID having been stolen had originally not even crossed my mind. The representative at the credit card company did mention the fact that because it was probably the same person who had gotten one thousand dollars from my account a few months ago, he must have had some form of identification, such as a driver's license with my information on it. That is when I became very alarmed.

I asked if I should file a police report, but they said it wasn't necessary. By this time, however, I had lost faith in the procedures of the credit card company, and was no longer inclined to take the company's advice. I immediately went down to my local police station, where I found the police reluctant to take my report. I insisted on filing the identity theft report there, anyway. To accomplish that, I once again had to prove that I was a victim of identity theft. This time, I had to prove it to the police. Fortunately, I still had my statement from back in October when I had disputed the thousand dollar charge, and that seemed to be sufficient for the police.

Many officers are reluctant to take identity theft reports, for the simple reason that those police reports tend to be vague and difficult to comprehend. Years ago, police reports were as simple as, "Someone broke into my car and stole my radio."

In this Internet age, a police report more likely goes something like this: "I opened my statement and found that someone in Chicago had withdrawn five hundred dollars from my account."

The officer probably knows nothing about Chicago. He can't go there hoping to find a bad guy with the money. To further complicate matters, the credit card company has already paid the victim, who then gets on with his life.

This is when my "What Do I Do Now" journey started. I learned so much during the process, that I thought I would share it with you. Maybe it will help you avoid becoming an identity theft victim, or at least be more informed about what to do if you ever have the misfortune of becoming such a victim.

CHAPTER 2

POLICE INVOLVEMENT

TWO weeks after filing the police report, a police detective from a nearby city phoned me. He had come across my personal information while searching the home of a local criminal. He offered to meet with me to go over the case.

During the interview he showed me a picture of the criminal on a driver's license that had *my* information on it. The criminal had not only created a fake ID for himself, but also one for his girlfriend.

I have never felt so violated in my entire life.

It is not uncommon for investigators to find huge stashes of personal identifying information, ranging from driver's licenses to bank account numbers, or credit card statements. Thieves store this information on paper, computer hard drives, data cards, cell phones, or on the magnetic strip on the back of someone's credit card.

Because search warrants are usually obtained with regard to drugs, gangs, or homicides, investigators often overlook personal identifying information during the search of a suspect's home.

It turned out that my information had been stolen from the escrow office where the transaction for the purchase of my home had taken place. They had everything; every piece of my information—including my credit reports and personal data—was in a binder they had seized at the suspect's house.

Interestingly enough, sixteen other individuals had their IDs stolen in that office, but none wanted to get involved with the police investigation, because all they cared about was that their credit card companies had credited the money back to them for the unauthorized charges. That was not enough for me though. I wanted to know more, and if possible, I wanted to pursue the criminals.

I learned so much from my direct involvement with the police.

The detective told me I was very lucky that he had discovered my information during an unrelated arrest. At least the thief no longer had access to it. But my mind was still not at ease.

I remained very involved with that police department for the whole year following the arrest of the criminal who had stolen my ID. At some point I learned that he had gotten out of jail for reasons that could not be discussed. All my worries re-surfaced, but at least this time I was prepared. I knew that it was going to be difficult for him to strike again. After all, it had taken *me* three hours to get a cell phone because of the freeze on my credit.

We will cover more details on police reports in Chapter 7.

CHAPTER 3

HOW YOUR ID GETS STOLEN

ACCORDING to the Federal Trade Commission, one in four people get their IDs stolen, and these are some ways it happens:

1.   **Dumpster Diving.** They rummage through trash looking for bills or other papers that contain your personal information.

2.   **Skimming.** They steal credit and debit card details by scanning the card using special storage devices (skimmers) when processing your card.

There are three common places where skimmers are used by criminals:

a.   Gas Stations
b.   ATMs
c.   Retail Establishments

We will cover more on how to watch out for skimmers in chapter 5.

3.   **Phising.** They pretend to be financial institutions or companies. They send e-mails, spams or pop-up messages that appear on your computer, or they could just call you and ask for your information over the phone. Their motive is to get you to reveal your personal information.

4. **Changing your address.** By placing a change of address at the post office, the thief has your mail delivered to his address. The post office will deliver your billing statements to another location, if the thieves have placed a change of address on your behalf. We cover more on this in chapter 5.

5. "**Old-fashioned stealing**." They steal wallets, purses, and mail that could contain bank and credit card statements, pre-approved credit offers, checks, and tax information. They steal personal records from employers (i.e. escrow offices, financial institutions) or bribe employees who have access.

6. **Other places.** Your doctor, accountant, lawyer, dentist, school, place of work, health insurance carrier, bank, and many others have your identifying information. Unscrupulous employees could potentially use your personal information, or sell it to someone else for criminal purposes.

The list goes on and on. Let's not forget that these crooks could even be working within the actual credit card company you contact when your ID gets stolen.

Chapter 4

What to Do If Your Identity Is Stolen

THIS is where things get complicated. If you find out your identity or your wallet was stolen, and you think you are safe, because you canceled your credit cards and put a "stop" on your checking account—think again. Once identity thieves have all your personal identifying information, they can make a fake ID and open new accounts or credit lines.

Crooks can buy a car and even get a traffic ticket in your name.

As mentioned in the previous chapter, the thief can submit an address change to divert your mail to wherever they like, so they could potentially have a lot more information than you can imagine. While on that subject, it is worth mentioning that in an effort to warn you of such actions, the post office now sends a "Move Validation Letter" to both the old and new addresses when a change is filed. The letter requests that you call an "800" number if you did not file the change. Therefore, it is important not to just throw away letters sent to you by the post office.

Remember that no one cares about your credit as much as you do.

Once the thieves have become you, they can buy homes, get loans, purchase goods, and do all that you can do—and more.

So be aggressive and proactive.
This is your credit, your livelihood,
your future. Take it seriously.

What to do

1.   Contact your creditors immediately by phone *and* in writing.

2.   Close any accounts that have been tampered with or established fraudulently by following the steps below:

    a.   Call the security or fraud department of each credit card where an account was opened or changed without your approval. Follow up in writing with copies of supporting documents.

    b.   Ask that old accounts be processed as "Account Closed" at the Consumer's Request. If you do not mention that, by default, the request will be reported to the credit bureaus as "card stolen or lost" which means *you* were irresponsible and careless with your information. In other words the blame is on *you,* and not on the fact that you were a *victim* of ID theft. That will have a negative reflection on your account.

    c.   Get verification in writing that the

disputed accounts have been closed and the fraudulent debts discharged. Every time you close an account you are given a reference number as a form of verification that the account has in fact been closed. Record any reference numbers that are given to you over the telephone.

d. Bear in mind that credit grantors might ask you to fill out and notarize fraud affidavits. That is a costly and time-consuming process. Be aware that the law does not require that a notarized affidavit be provided to creditors. A written statement and a copy of the police report should be sufficient.

e. Keep copies of all documents and records of your conversations including time, date, name, and the phone number and/or extension number of the person processing your requests. Do not ever throw away these documents. You never know when you will need them in the future. You never know when the thieves will resurface.

3. Go to the police station and file a police report in the jurisdiction where you believe your ID was stolen. You will need to complete a form, and the police will ask you some questions.

You then have to carefully review the report and sign it if you find that it is accurate. If it is not accurate, clarify the changes that need to be made to the report before you sign it. This report documents the fact that you are a victim of ID theft. In the event that someone assumes your identity and commits a crime or any other malicious act that makes you liable, the existence of a previously filed police report can vindicate you later. Make sure you bring documentation that proves you are an ID theft victim. It could be something as simple as a disputed charge on your credit card.

Your credit card company will probably tell you not to bother with filing a police report— that they will handle everything themselves. Do not believe it. Insist on filing the police report. Remember that you need to take matters into your own hands. Some creditors will want proof of the crime, and that is when the police report will be invaluable.

4.   To stop the thieves from using your credit, you can either place a freeze or a fraud alert on your credit by calling all three credit bureaus: Experian, Equifax, and Transunion (see below for details). Some credit bureaus require the request for the freeze to be in writing, which makes it more time consuming. However,

merely putting a fraud alert on your credit may not be good enough. A fraud alert only lasts for ninety days and is easier to get around than an actual credit freeze.

In most states:

- Placing a fraud alert or freeze on your credit entitles you to free copies of your credit reports.

- Proving that you are an ID theft victim can be accomplished by simply submitting your police report.

- Placing the freeze is free of charge once you have proven that you are an ID theft victim.

Bear in mind that putting a freeze on your credit will also make it difficult for *you* to access your own credit. Consider this though: How many credit cards do you apply for each year, and how many homes or cars do you buy? Although inconvenient, a freeze stops a suspect dead in his tracks if he is planning to get credit in your name.

Once you have placed the freeze on your credit, you will be provided with a PIN number. When you require access to your credit, you can call your credit card bureaus provide your PIN number, and have the freeze lifted temporarily—for as short as twenty-four hours, or for up to thirty days— and then the freeze will be automatically reinstated. Again, placing a fraud alert can entitle you to free copies of your credit reports.

You can also sign up with certain well-known companies to alert you through email or phone anytime there are unusual activities on your account. Some of these companies charge as little as $9.95 per month. I have this service, and I think it is worth every penny. You can also check with your financial institution. They also offer credit monitoring.

To place an alert or a freeze on your credit, contact the credit bureaus at:

Equifax:

http://www.equifax.com

To report fraud:
P.O. Box 105069
Atlanta, GA 30348
(800) 525-6285

To order credit report:
P.O. Box 740241
Atlanta, GA 30374
(800) 685-1111

Experian:

http://www.experian.com/fraud

To report fraud:
P.O. Box 949
Allen, TX 75013-0949
(888) 397-3742
(888) Experian

To order credit report: (888)397-3742

Transunion:

http://www.Transunion.com

To report fraud:
P.O. Box 6790
Fullerton, CA 92634
(800) 680-7289

To order credit report:
P.O. Box 390
Springfield, PA 19064-0390
(800) 916-8800

5. Inform the Social Security Administration by calling: (800) 269-0271

Also, request a copy of your Earnings and Benefits Statement at least once a year and check it for accuracy. Remember that people could be working under your social security number.

6. Contact the Department of Motor Vehicles (DMV). The DMV usually has a fraud hotline. Otherwise, you can go to their website to find out where you need to file a report.

Obtain the DMV phone number for your state, and place it below:

Ask the DMV to find out whether another driver's license has been issued in your name. You can also put an alert on your license.

Fill out the DMV's complaint form to begin the fraud investigation process. Be sure to send supporting documents with the complaint form to the nearest DMV investigation office.

You may need to change your driver's license number if someone is using yours as identification.

Bear in mind that even having done all of the above, the suspect could always get a fake ID with your information on it. When I contacted DMV I was told that the fake IDs these days are so good that even DMV investigators have a hard time identifying them!

Consider placing a P.O. Box address on your actual driver's license. In the event that your license is lost, this will prevent the suspect from learning your home address.

7.   Contact the Federal Trade Commission (FTC) by:

http://www.ftc.gov/idtheft
http://www.consumer.gov/idtheft

Mail:
Bureau of Consumer Protection
Consumer Response Center/Identity
Theft Clearinghouse
600 Pennsylvania Ave N.W.
Washington, DC 20580
(877) ID-THEFT (877) 438-4338

"By sharing your identity theft complaint with the FTC, you will provide important information that can help law enforcement officials across the nation track down identity thieves and stop them. The FTC can refer victims' complaints to other government agencies and companies for further action, as well as investigate companies for violations of laws the agency enforces.

Additionally, you can provide a printed copy of your online complaint form to the police to incorporate into their report. The printed FTC ID Theft Complaint, in conjunction with the police report, can constitute an Identity Theft Report and entitle you to certain protections. This Identity Theft Report can be used to (1) permanently block fraudulent information from appearing on your credit report; (2) ensure that debts do not reappear on your credit report; (3) prevent a company from continuing to collect debts that result from identity theft; and (4) place an extended fraud alert on your credit report ..." **—Source: FTC Web site.**

Once you have the ID Theft Affidavit obtained from the Federal Trade Commission you can use it as a supporting document in your communications with the credit bureaus, financial institutions, or credit grantors. Again by reporting to the FTC you may be able to help law enforcement officials across the country with their investigations.

8.   Contact Chex Systems:
Let them know your ID has been stolen. This company might be able to prevent the thief from having the ability to open a bank account using your personal information.

http://www.chexhelp.com

ChexSystems, Inc.
Consumer Relations
7805 Hudson Road, Suite 100
Woodbury, MN 55125
Phone number: (800) 428-9623
Fax number: (602) 659-2197

9.   Contact the U.S. Postal Inspection Service. Because most identity theft involves the U.S. Mail, the U.S. Postal Inspection Service has taken the lead in investigating these crimes. Postal Inspectors have jurisdiction to investigate and enforce more than two hundred federal statutes involving the U.S. mail.

10. To speed up the process of communicating with creditors and financial institutions, create a generic letter addressing the creditor, financial institution, or whomever you are disputing a charge with, and just fill in the blanks as you go. Make sure the letter includes the following information:

Your name
Address
Phone number

Date

Account number/Reference number

Dear Mr/Mrs/Ms_____:

I am writing to you to inform you that I have been a victim of identity theft, and I did not incur the expenses on the above mentioned account (or that you did not open that account—whichever applies).

I have also filed an Identity Theft report with the police department in the city of _____ with case number____, and I have enclosed a copy of that report for your reference. Should you have any further questions regarding this report, please contact the police department at (Provide contact information for the police department) _____.

ID theft could have some other consequences.

False Civil and Criminal Judgments.

Sometimes victims of ID theft are wrongfully accused of crimes committed by the imposter. If you are informed of such a situation contact the court where the judgment was entered, and report that you have been a victim of ID theft. If you are being prosecuted for criminal charges contact the State Department of Justice, and ask how to clear your name.

If you feel that you need to seek legal help and you want to speak to an attorney, find one who specializes in consumer law and the Fair Credit Reporting Act.

You may also consult a lawyer if you feel that creditors are not cooperating with you to remove fraudulent entries from your credit report, or if they are simply neglecting your requests.

Again, you can sign up with certain companies that will monitor your credit on a daily basis. These companies check information from all three national credit reporting agencies. They will notify you via e-mail or regular mail of changes such as new accounts, public records, inquiries, and changes of address. So you will also be able to see whether any of the above has been detected in your credit report.

Remember that receiving inquiries from institutions you never had an affiliation with may signify that someone has stolen your identity and is using it to apply for loans in your name.

CHAPTER 5

HOW TO PREVENT IDENTITY THEFT

CREDIT CARDS

1. Do not sign the back of your credit cards. Instead, write clearly "Check Photo ID." The clerk will most likely pay attention and ask for it. If your credit card company provides you the option of having your picture on the card, *do so*.

2. Some credit cards allow you to have a PIN number or password when calling to access your information. Make sure to set that up.

3. Do not provide your personal information or credit card number to anyone over the phone unless *you* have initiated the call.

4. Do not give your personal information via the mail or on the internet unless you are absolutely certain you know who you are dealing with.

5. Use a cross-cut paper shredder to shred credit card convenience checks and pre-approved credit offers if you are not planning to use them. Also shred all other financial documents and paperwork containing personal information. Simply tearing up these documents is not sufficient.

6. Always collect your receipts from credit card, ATM, and check transactions.

7.   When you give away your credit card to pay for dinner at a restaurant, make sure you get the same card back. The waiter could switch your card with someone else's card that looks the same as yours. You may only find out when it is too late. The waitress may run it through a card-reading device or take a photo of it with her cell phone. If that happens, you will later realize the actual cost of the meal after you discover an unknown internet transaction that occurred on the other side of the world.

8.   When you receive e-mails from supposedly a financial institution or well-known sites involved in financial transactions, pay attention to the URL (web address) once you have clicked on it. For example, if you believe that you are opening up an e-mail sent by Wells Fargo, make certain that once you are on the site the URL still reads Wells Fargo—and not some weird URL that is designed to make you believe you are on the Wells Fargo site, when in fact on a site run by criminals. Here is one example:

>   http://www.members.axion.net ~ rod/.
>   Wells.Fargo.com

CHECKS

1.   If you are using checks to pay your credit
       card bill, do not write the entire credit card
       number on the check. Just the last four digits
       are sufficient. That is all the credit card
       company needs to locate your account.

2.   Do not print your driver's license number,
       your middle name, or telephone number on
       your checks unless it is absolutely required.
       In other words do not volunteer that infor-
       mation. Also, with today's technology most
       retailers are able to verify your check at the
       point of sale, and such information is not
       required.

SOCIAL SECURITY NUMBER

1.   Do not carry your social security card with
       you. Do not write that number on your
       checks and never give it out unless you abso-
       lutely have to. Always object to the use of
       your social security number (SSN) and ask
       to use another identifier instead. Businesses
       should by now be aware that they should be
       using a form of identification other than SSN,
       so this won't be the first time they've had this
       request from customers. Always requesting
       another identifier may help the company
       prioritize making the switch to another iden-
       tification system.

While we are on the subject of SSN, did you know that your child's SSN could be stolen? By the time she is ready to start college she can owe thousands of dollars in student loans, car payments, credit cards, and other debts. Check credit reports on your child's SSN at least once a year.

DMV

If you are expecting your driver's license or ID card and have not received it within the allotted time, contact the DMV and inquire about the delay.

Skimming

Look out for skimmers. A gas station skimmer is usually attached to the pump or to a pay-point. The device is attached on top of the regular reader in a way that your card will pass through the skimmer before entering the legitimate reader.

An ATM skimmer is placed on top of the keypad to record your PIN number. These devices are placed for twenty-four hours before the thieves remove them and upload the data onto a computer. The information is read in a Word document, and includes your card number, name, expiration date, and PIN number. The skimmer will re-encode new cards using card encoders that are readily available on popular internet auction sites.

***Skimmers can steal tens to hundreds of thou-
sands in a matter of hours.***

While checking your statement, if you find that
someone has withdrawn money from your account at
some obscure location, you have probably been hit by
a skimmer.

At retail establishments, the criminals will physically
run your card (as they would for a normal transaction,
i.e. for a soda at a gas station) and then re-swipe it
onto their own reader, which stores your card information. That information can then be uploaded onto
a cell phone, or any other device that stores data.
Later, it can be emailed to a co-conspirator. Your card
information is then re-encoded onto new cards, which
are used all over the world within hours, and usually
while you are asleep. Bottom line: Do not let your card
leave your sight.

To prevent becoming a victim of skimming, check
the ATM before using it; look for anything suspicious.
Suspects usually stick their devices to the ATMs and
pay-points/check outs, so check to see whether the
card reader or keypad look loose. Check to see if they
move or come off with gentle pressure. Check for a
pin-hole camera above the keypad. Notice if someone
is watching the ATM in a suspicious manner, and if so,
leave without using that ATM.

If you notice any of these things, call the police and show them what you suspect.

General

Secure your personal information in a safe place, especially if you have roommates, if you employ outside help, or if you are having work done in your house.

Make sure you keep PIN numbers in a safe place. Losing them could be disastrous.

Never use an obvious password, such as your birth date, mother's maiden name, the last four digits of your social security number, or your pet's name.

Make copies of every card that you carry in your wallet; *that means both sides of every card.* Keep these copies in a safe but readily available place.

If your wallet gets stolen, the process is much faster if you have the phone number to your credit card company as well as your account number. Save the phone number for your credit card company into your cell phone.

In today's world it is almost inevitable to do finances on-line, and we have no control over what goes on at the banking level. However, what we can do as individuals is to watch over our own transactions. Check your bank and credit card accounts on-line at least once a week. Make a ritual out of it, and look for charges that you know you did not make.

When leaving your car with valet parking give them only your car key. Remember to remove your house keys or any other keys. Most car companies will now provide you with a "Valet Key" when you purchase a car.

If you ever get denied for credit, don't just let it go. Investigate it. Your credit might have been affected by activities that you did not authorize.

As mentioned before, take it very seriously when bills do not arrive as expected, or when you receive calls or letters about purchases you did not make. These could be the first signs of a looming ID catastrophe.

Never just be satisfied with the credit card company simply crediting your account and reassuring you that you will not be responsible for the charges. Look into it further.

> *You can also limit what goes into your mail box by signing up with Direct Marketing Association (DMA) at:*

> http://www.e-mps.org
> or http://www.the-dma.org
> or go to:
> http://www.optoutprescreen.com

By receiving less mail with your information on it you limit the thieves' access to your personal data.

Pay attention to the mail you receive. For example, in most states, each time you buy, sell, or take out a loan on your property, the county sends you a copy of the recorded document. This gives you a chance to review the document to be sure it is correct, and that no one is conducting transactions on your house without your knowledge. The copy is sent to the property address and any other address on file at the County Assessor's Office. If you did not initiate the transaction, contact your state's Department of Consumer Affairs immediately.

Find out their number in your state and write it in the space below.

_____.

The Department of Consumer Affairs Real Estate Fraud and Information Program can also help you if:

a.   Your name was forged on a real-estate document.

b.   Your home was sold without your knowledge. (Believe it or not, it does happen).

c.   Title was transferred without your knowledge.

Mailboxes tend to be common points of compromise for victims. The sad part is that most people don't realize their mail has been stolen until it is too late. The thieves mainly concentrate on apartment and condo complexes with mass mailbox units. He will break the single rear access lock, and in one swoop, he has the mail belonging to ten to thirty victims.

They will also target those single mailboxes with red flags on them. These mailboxes sit outside of many homes. When you have put your bills, checks, etcetera in the box, the suspect goes down the street, taking mail (personal information) from everyone's mailboxes. Thieves usually will show up late on a Sunday when streets are least crowded. If you suspect that your mail has been stolen, report it immediately to your local postmaster or nearest postal inspector. You will be asked to complete a form.

This will also help postal inspectors determine whether the theft of your mail is isolated or is part of a larger mail-theft operation in your neighborhood.

Always put outgoing mail in a secure place or pay bills online, using an encrypted site.

Because your mail box could be filled with pre-approved credit card offers, you can avoid receiving them by contacting the following:

(888)5optout
or
www.optoutprescreen.com

As mentioned earlier, you can obtain a free copy of your credit report to keep an eye on the activities by visiting the website:

http://www.AnnualCreditReport.com

Call (877) 322-8228 or write to them at:

Annual Credit Report Request Service
P.O. Box 105281
Atlanta, GA 30348-5281

The law requires each of the major nationwide consumer reporting companies, Equifax, Experian, and Transunion to provide you a free copy of your credit report once a year. Therefore, obtain one from Equifax in February, one from Experian in June, and one from Transunion in October. Even though this might affect your credit score by a few points, it is well worth protecting it from plunging down as a result of unauthorized activities.

CHAPTER 6

TRAVELING ABROAD

I will never forget the feeling when I got off the Metro in Paris, and something told me that my wallet had been stolen. I froze and told my friend, "My wallet is gone." He looked at me and asked, "How do you know? You haven't even looked inside your purse." I prayed that my feeling was wrong, but it was not.

I searched, but my red wallet had been stolen from my purse as I had stood among the crowd at the Metro Station. I had nothing—no money, no ATM cards, and no credit cards. Thankfully my passport was in the pocket of my purse and had not been taken.

> *Never keep your*
> *wallet and passport together.*

Because the vacation was supposed to be on me, my friend had not brought any credit cards with him. We were literally stranded. Luckily, I had a phone card. We rushed over to a pay phone, and I called my brother in the U.S., who in turn called the credit card companies. My friend managed to go to the police station, but because our train to Nice was leaving in less than twenty minutes, and we had no money to buy more tickets, they said to do the police report once we got to Nice.

> *That police report saved me*
> *a lot of trouble later on.*

From the time I paid for the tickets, got on and off at the very next station, and realized my wallet was gone, no more than fifteen minutes had elapsed. To get to the pay phone and have my brother contact the credit card company was another fifteen minutes.

Within half an hour, the thieves had already charged over $5,500.00 on one credit card at a furniture store. Not only that, but they tried to run my second credit card for the same exact transaction. The first credit card company should have questioned this. I had never made large purchases on that credit card before, and I most certainly had never bought furniture in France.

Fortunately, my second credit card had denied the same exact purchase, and I was able to cancel the card in time.

However, over a month after I returned to the U.S., the very same financial institution that had *denied* the $5,500 purchase and *had been informed in time* that the card had been stolen, called me to question some charges that were being made in Spain.

Amazingly, this credit card company was allowing small amounts to be withdrawn by the thieves, even though that credit card had been reported as stolen and therefore *cancelled*.

Meanwhile the first credit card company that had *allowed* the $5,500 furniture purchase to go through claimed that the French shopkeeper had checked for my ID, and it was shown. Obviously, that was because they did have my driver's license as well. Having said that, what are the chances that the person who stole my wallet really looked like me?

I tried to convince the credit card company that the shopkeeper must have been involved, or that the furniture store business was just a front.

The shopkeeper had also tried to run my other credit card for the same exact amount, but it had been denied. Interestingly, the time of transaction on this card was *after* the first transaction had been approved. But the credit card company did not want to hear that. It was not worth their time to investigate such matters. They allowed the thieves to get away with the crime and put it down as just another write-off. It is cheaper to re-reimburse the customer than to pursue a legal case.

It is up to you to protect yourself.

So when traveling:

Take only one or at maximum two credit cards with you. If taking two, keep them in separate places.

If you do not take a cell phone with you, make sure you purchase a calling card from the country you are staying in, and make certain you know how to use it. They are usually sold at newspaper stands.

Make copies of your passport and of everything in your wallet. Leave one set of the copies with someone you trust back home, and take one set with you. Be sure to carry the set of copies in a different location than your wallet or purse.

Don't carry purses with a strap; they could easily be snatched or cut. If you do, make sure your purse not only zips up, but has a flap going over the zipper. Always wear the purse so the flap is towards your body and not away from it.

Men should never place their wallet in the back pocket, even if the pocket buttons up. Carry your wallet in a deep front pocket that has a zipper or buttons.

Do not carry all of your cash on you or in your wallet. You can always leave some in the safe in your room, and put some in a money pouch around your waist or neck, making sure you hide it under clothing, as these could also be snatched off.

Be aware of your surroundings. Constantly look behind and around you. Do not place your purse, phone, or camera on the chair next to you or on the table. When you want to use the bathroom, give your purse to the person accompanying you.

Do not act like a typical tourist by constantly looking at maps. Try to be discreet and less obvious, otherwise you are only setting yourself up as a target and distracting yourself from your belongings and surroundings. Plan the route in advance by looking at maps in your hotel room or in other places where it won't be so obvious. Jot down notes from a map to remind you of directions and discretely glance at your notes if necessary.

If you rent a car always keep the doors locked. In a split second a thief can simply open the back door and take your belongings from the backseat. Or a thief could intentionally cause an "accident" with you. Usually the criminal will be on a motorbike, hitting the front tire for example, and while you are being distracted, an accomplice will steal your belongings from the back seat if your doors are not locked.

While doing the police report in Nice, one of the police officers told me that if you do not lock your car, the thieves sometimes just open the doors, drag you out, and hijack the car. They can tell by stickers or certain license plates that the car is a rental.

CHAPTER 7

KNOW YOUR RIGHTS

THE Fair Credit Reporting Act (FCRA) grants consumers important rights regarding consumer credit, credit files, and related matters. Some of these are:

1.   You have the legal right to know your credit score. For a fee, you may request your credit score at:

    http://www.AnnualCreditReport.com

2.   You can dispute inaccurate information with the Consumer Reporting Agencies. If you tell a consumer reporting agency that your file has inaccurate information, the agency *must* take certain steps to investigate your claim.

3.   Inaccurate information must be corrected or deleted. A consumer reporting agency must remove or correct information verified as inaccurate, usually within thirty days after you dispute it.

    It also states that if you think a bill you have received is in error, you may notify the creditor in writing within sixty days. The creditor must either correct the bill or send you an explanation within ninety days.

4.   Victims of identity theft have new rights under the FCRA. For more information visit:

http://www.ftc.gov/credit

or write to:

Consumer Response Center
Federal Trade Commission
600 Pennsylvania Ave. N.W.
Washington, DC 20580
(877) 382-4357

The Federal Trade Commission says there were nearly 10 million identity theft victims in the United States in 2008. The losses cost businesses and financial institutions $48 billion and cost individuals $5 billion in expenses correcting the damage and proving they were victims rather than culprits.

Can you change your social security number if you are a victim of identity theft?

In most cases this is a bad idea. You have had that number for many years, and it is attached to many documents, including your credit report and various other private and governmental documents.

Changing your social security number will cause incredible problems within the Social Security Administration. Your credit reports with your old social security number will be attached to the reports with the new number. This will look very suspicious to creditors and employers, and will likely cause further problems in proving you to be the victim instead of the imposter.

What if the police won't take a report?

Many police departments are reluctant to write a report on this type of crime. The officers may tell you that *you* are not the victim, and that the credit grantor, who lost the money *is*.

They normally want the report to come from the creditor, who often will not cooperate, because it is not cost-effective for them to spend the time and labor assisting the police. They may have already lost thousands of dollars and are not willing to lose any more. But if the creditor won't prosecute, you must insist that the police make a report.

Refusing to file a police report is very unfair to you, given the potential difficulties that may arise later if you have to prove that you have been the victim. Having said that, the police report can be extremely helpful in such circumstances, even though ID victims are not necessarily a priority concern for the police. There is no doubt that this reluctance to take police reports in cases of identity theft has to change, but for now, that is often the situation that identity theft victims encounter.

If you feel as if you are getting nowhere, request to speak to the head of the fraud unit or the white-crime unit of the police department in the counties or cities where the fraudulent accounts were opened.

If fraudulent accounts were opened all around the U.S., you may be able to get the FBI involved.

Don't be afraid to call your local police detective. It is common for the fraud desk to be inundated with cases. Sometimes a phone call or e-mail from the victim will be enough to prioritize your case, and ensure that the correct follow-up is conducted.

You may have to accept that the thief who stole your ID may never be caught, but at least you may discover how he obtained your information, and you can make sure to never allow it to be stolen again.

ID theft is the fastest growing crime, and even though you may receive your money back from the credit card companies, you should still protect yourself from future hits. Victims often hope that they won't be targeted again; however, once the suspect has your information, he can withdraw money from your account months later. Go on the offensive. Do what is right.

CONCLUSION

YOUR credit is like a baby. You create it, nurture it, and make certain it is well maintained. It is hard work doing all of that, but at the end of the day it is worth it.

With good credit you can do so much: continue your education, buy your dream house, get your favorite car, start up a business, make investments, send your children to college, pay for their weddings, and lots more.

When you have a child, you make sure he gets vaccinations, regular check-ups, and is well-fed. Why not do the same with your credit? Check up on it regularly. Be proactive about protecting it, and have the right tools to fight with if it ever gets taken away from you.

In the U.S. we are constantly judged by our credit reports. Our credit reports affect buying a house, buying a car, applying for student loans, renting a place, purchasing goods, getting credit cards, the rate at which we get our loans, starting a business, opening a bank account, borrowing money, and many more activities depend upon how good our credit is. Your credit is the most important aspect of your financial life. Without it, you will face road blocks every step of the way. With it, the sky is the limit.

   Look After It.